STEM Junior
TECHNOLOGY

KINGFISHER
LONDON & NEW YORK

LONDON & NEW YORK

Text and design copyright © Toucan Books Ltd. 2020
Illustrations copyright © Simon Basher 2020
www.basherscience.com

First published 2020 in the United States by Kingfisher
120 Broadway, New York, NY 10271
Kingfisher is an imprint of Macmillan Children's Books, London
All rights reserved.

Author: Jonathan O'Callaghan
Consultants: Robin Ulster and James Denby
Editor: Anna Southgate
Designer: Leah Germann
Indexer: Marie Lorimer
Proofreader: Richard Beatty

Dedicated to Tom and Charlie

Distributed in the U.S. and Canada by Macmillan,
120 Broadway, New York, NY 10271

Library of Congress Cataloging-in-Publication Data has been applied for.

ISBN: 978-0-7534-7559-1 (Hardcover)
ISBN: 978-0-7534-7555-3 (Paperback)

Kingfisher books are available for special promotions and premiums.
For details contact: Special Markets Department, Macmillan, 120 Broadway,
New York, NY 10271

For more information, please visit www.kingfisherbooks.com

Printed in China
9 8 7 6 5 4 3 2 1
1TR/0420/WKT/UG/128MA

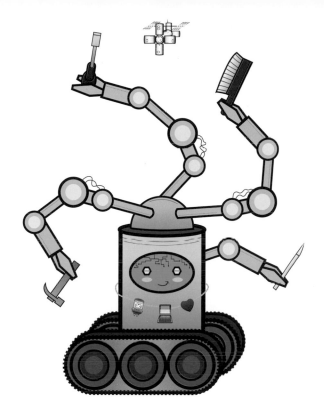

Contents

Technology Rules!   4

Home Buddies   6

Computer Crew   24

Super High-Tech Crew   44

Power Pals   62

Turbo Transporters   80

Glossary   94

Index   96

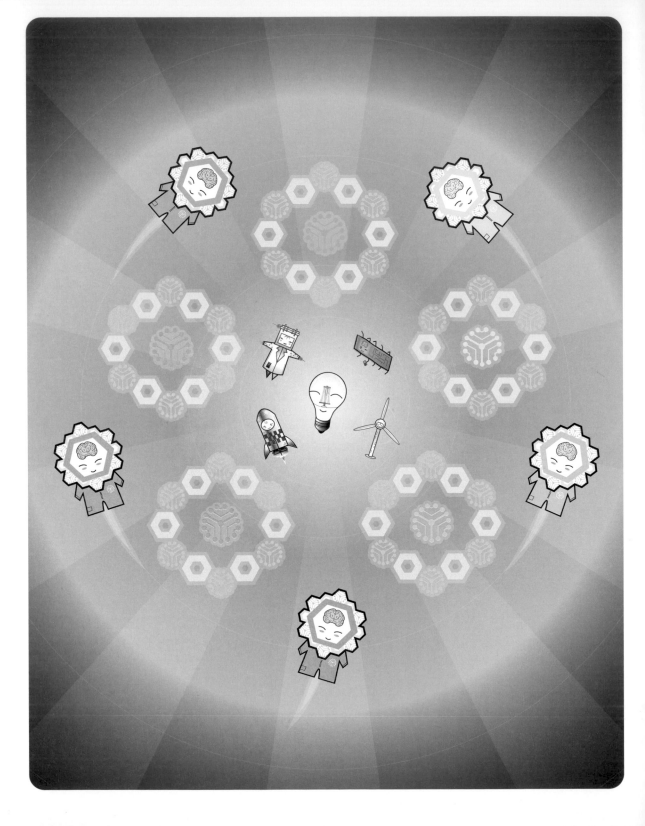

Technology Rules!

No, really. Without technology, we'd probably still be living in caves. Think about it. No cars, no electricity, no TV, no Internet, no *toilet*. Oh no! These are not happy thoughts. Thankfully, I know a bunch of techno wizards whom I'd like you to meet.

These super-talented types have helped create a world where you can turn a light on at night and make phone calls out in the open. You won't believe the amazing stories they have to tell. Like, who knew you could cut metal using a light beam or travel to faraway places without even leaving your couch? Come on, let's find out what they have to say.

Light Bulb

Toilet

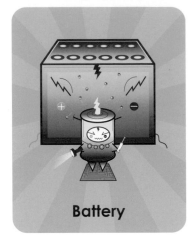

Battery

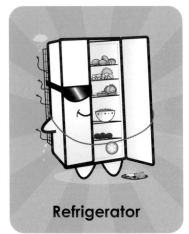

Refrigerator

Microwave Oven

Radio

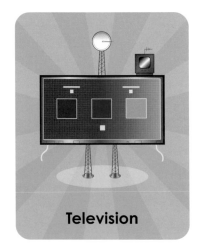

Television

Internet of Things

Home Buddies

What do you get up to at home? Maybe you watch TV or listen to the radio. Do you raid the refrigerator when you're hungry? You definitely turn the lights on when it gets dark. And, of course, you use the toilet every so often! These Home Buddies are household gadgets that you use all the time. But do you know how they all work? Well, they want to tell you for themselves. Read on, and get ready to have your mind blown!

Light Bulb
★ Great Glower

THE BIG IDEA

An electric lamp. It gives off light when switched on.

You've just gotten home and it's nighttime. How do you make things bright enough to see? Use me, Light Bulb! I shine a light with the flick of a switch that sends electricity flowing through me.

I often have a thin wire inside me called a filament. Switch me on and my filament heats up. It gets hotter and hotter until it starts to produce **particles** called photons. These carry light from the bulb to your eyes the moment you turn it on. Modern-day light bulbs use an electronic device called a light-emitting diode (LED) instead of a filament. They use much less energy to make light. I have a bright future!

- The world's biggest light bulb is 13 ft. (4 m) across; it sits atop a tower in honor of Thomas Edison, in Edison, New Jersey

- LEDs use over 75% less energy than regular light bulbs

SAY WHAT?

Particle: A tiny piece of matter, such as an atom (see page 94). Inside each atom are smaller particles called electrons and protons (see pages 94 and 95).

TECH LEGENDS

Many people say that American inventor Thomas Edison invented the light bulb in 1879, but British chemist Warren De La Rue came up with the idea almost 40 years earlier! It was expensive, though, and Edison made it much cheaper.

Toilet

★ Famous Flusher

THE BIG IDEA

A system that takes human waste away from the home. It connects to an underground **sewer.**

It's a dirty job, but how would you get rid of all that unwanted waste? You've seen a "flush" toilet, and campers will also know the pit toilet, which collects waste in a deep hole in the ground. I'm a fan of the flush myself . . .

You sit on my bowl, which has a tank above it. A pipe connects the two. Another pipe fills the tank with water. Press down on a handle (or push a button), and presto! Water gushes from the tank into the bowl, pushing your waste down the drainpipe and into the sewer. The tank fills up again, so I am always ready when you are — and squeaky clean!

- ◉ Toilets are sometimes called the "John," perhaps because of John Harington, who invented the flush toilet!

- ◉ On average, you go to the toilet 2,500 times every year

⚡ SAY WHAT? ⚡

Sewer: A network of large pipes that carries household waste to a place where it can be safely gotten rid of.

✳ TECH LEGENDS ✳

Englishman John Harington invented the modern flush toilet around 1590. He made it for Queen Elizabeth I, but the idea didn't fly. In 1775, English inventor Alexander Cumming improved the design using pipes and valves. That's when the flush toilet became popular.

Battery
★ Super Storer

THE BIG IDEA

A container that stores energy until it is needed. It generates electricity when connected to a circuit (see page 28).

Look, no plug! I'm a clever device that stores energy for later use. I come in different shapes and sizes, and I'm used to power up gadgets on the go: remote-controlled toys, your electric toothbrush, and more.

I have two metal ends, called "terminals." One is positive, the other negative. Between them is a powdery chemical mixture. Connect me to my pal Circuit — say, inside a flashlight — and electricity runs from one end of me to the other. The **atoms** in the chemicals react with my metal ends, and this produces the power needed to get a gizmo working. But don't overdo it! The more I'm used, the weaker I get.

- Italian physicist Alessandro Volta invented the battery in 1799

- The world's biggest battery is located in Australia

- A battery in Oxford, England, has lasted for almost 200 years; it rings a bell

SAY WHAT?

Atom: A tiny piece of matter, made of even tinier particles. Everything you see around you is made up of atoms (even you).

✳ APPLYING SCIENCE ✳

You're probably familiar with small batteries, but big ones exist, too — for example, the type of battery that helps start a car's engine. These normally rely on liquid chemicals, but they work in much the same way as the little batteries that you see at home.

Refrigerator
★ Cool Customer

THE BIG IDEA

A large container for storing food and drinks at cold temperatures. It keeps them fresh for longer.

I'm a cool customer that hogs half the food in your kitchen! Hey, don't worry, it's safe with me. I'm just using my low temperatures to keep nasty **bacteria** at bay. I keep food from rotting, saving it for another day!

A clever coolant helps me stay chilled. It travels from my top to my bottom inside a zigzagging pipe. As the pressure changes, it turns from liquid to gas and removes the heat from inside me. At my bottom, the gas is squeezed tight to make it hot. It runs up my back, releasing heat through a metal grid as it goes. It then turns back to liquid, and around it goes again!

◉ Before refrigerators, people used cool rooms and ice to chill food

◉ The ideal temperature in a refrigerator is 35° F–38° F (1.7° C–3.3° C)

SAY WHAT?

Bacteria: Super-tiny living things that can be found everywhere. Some help you digest your food, some cause diseases, and others can make food go bad.

TECH LEGENDS

American inventor Oliver Evans was the first person to come up with the idea for a refrigerator, in 1805. It wasn't until 1857 that they were used to store food, thanks to James Harrison, a Scotsman living in Australia. Refrigerators weren't used in homes until 1927!

Microwave Oven

★ Speedy Chef

THE BIG IDEA

A device that heats or cooks food by blasting it with **radiation**.

While Refrigerator keeps its cool in the kitchen, I'm a hot-headed type with a talent for speedy heating. If you need food defrosted or reheated — or just want to pop some corn — I'll deliver in no time.

I have a tube called a magnetron inside me that produces microwaves. This little gizmo uses electricity to generate a type of radiation that bounces around inside me (my waves!). When they hit food, my waves cause the atoms in the food to vibrate. The food heats up from the inside, cooking in less time than it takes in a regular oven. Just set my timer and before you know it, BING!

- The type of radiation used in a microwave oven is also used in speed cameras and cell phones

- The microwave was originally called a Radarange because the magnetron was used in developing radar

SAY WHAT?

Radiation: Energy that moves from one place to another. It is described as traveling in "waves." Radio waves, light waves, and microwaves are all forms of radiation.

TECH LEGEND

The microwave was invented by American Percy Spencer in 1945, but he discovered the technology by accident! Working in a lab, he had a magnetron switched on, and a chocolate bar in his pocket melted. He realized the microwaves had "cooked" it.

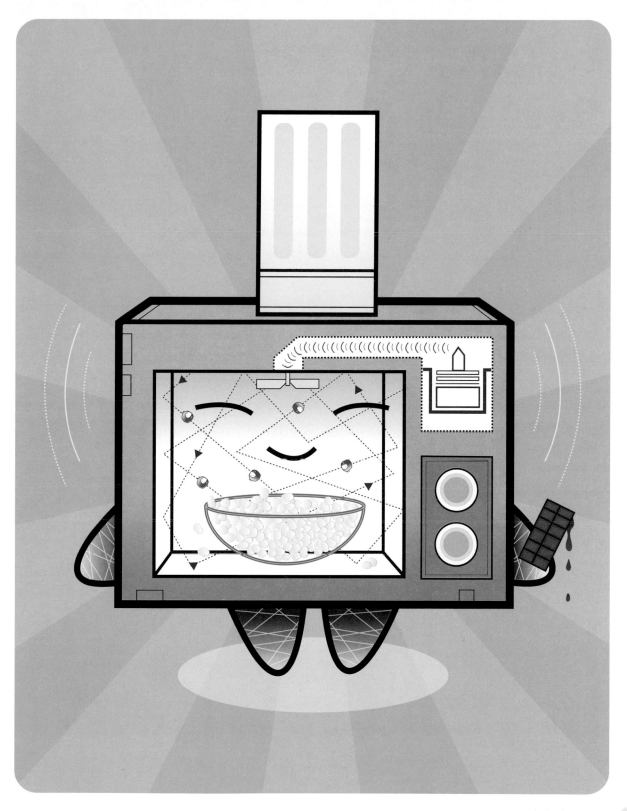

Radio
★ Talkative Type

THE BIG IDEA

A method of sending sound, such as music, and other information through the air or through space.

I'll talk, you listen! Just like Microwave, my technology relies on a kind of radiation. My invisible waves carry news bulletins, rock songs, stories, and more. They travel across huge distances, reaching many people at the same time, as long as they each have a device called a radio set!

The radio set in your house collects my waves from distant **transmitters**, which send them out in a big circle. On receiving my waves, your radio set converts them into sound for all to hear! Just tune in to your favorite radio station and away you go. It's music to my ears!

- ◉ Italian Guglielmo Marconi invented radio communication in the 1890s

- ◉ The first radio broadcast took place on Christmas Eve in 1906

- ◉ There are about 44,000 radio stations around the world

SAY WHAT?

Transmitter: A device that uses a metal rod or wire called an antenna to send out radio waves. A radio set uses an antenna to receive the signals.

✱ APPLYING SCIENCE ✱

Radio waves can travel such great distances that scientists use them to communicate with spacecraft. Satellites orbiting Earth and probes on distant planets use radio waves to send information to Earth.

Television

★ Picture Perfect

THE BIG IDEA

A screen that can display movies and TV shows. The images are sent via a transmitter, cable, or satellite.

You know me! I'm the great entertainer, that magic screen that delivers a cartoon, a movie, or tomorrow's weather as a full-blown audio and visual display (that's sound and pictures to you). You can call me TV!

Old versions of me used a picture tube. On receiving a signal, my pal Circuit split the signal into red, blue, and green colors. Fired from the picture tube onto the back of my screen, they combined to make the images people saw. Today's liquid crystal display (LCD) screens use thousands of **pixels** to do this, with tiny light switches changing their colors. Get the picture?

- ◉ The first TVs were black and white; color came from the 1950s onward

- ◉ One single pixel can change into millions of colors

- ◉ Today, almost four out of five households in the world have a TV

⚡ **SAY WHAT?** ⚡

Pixel: A tiny part of a display that can change color. Lots of pixels combine to make a larger picture.

✳ TECH LEGENDS ✳

Scottish inventor John Logie Baird first displayed moving images in January 1926. Starting in 1927, American pioneer Philo Farnsworth and others developed an electronic television that would eventually be used in homes around the world.

Internet of Things
★ Everything Online

What if Refrigerator could tell you when you've run out of milk? How about if Microwave could reorder popcorn when you're down to the last kernel? Let me help! I'm the well-connected type.

My pals call me IoT, and I'm the idea that all Home Buddies will soon be connected to the Internet (and to each other). It means they'll be able to send and receive information to make them more useful to you. Of course, I need help from networking superhero Internet to make this happen — you'll find out more in the next chapter.

- Around two billion websites can be reached online

- More than half of the world's population uses the Internet

- By 2022, some 29 billion devices will be connected to the Internet

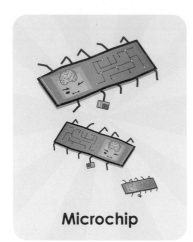

Microchip

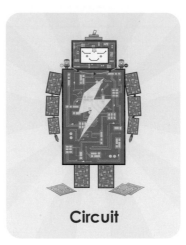

Circuit

Cable

Computer

Game Console

Touch Screen

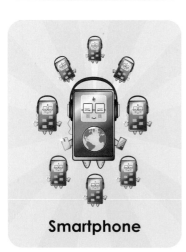

Smartphone

Internet

Wi-Fi

Computer Crew

There is a chance you use a computer every day, but you probably have NO IDEA how it works! Well, that's okay. When you think of the hundreds of things a computer can do, no wonder the technology seems complex! Do you know what the Internet is? Or what goes on when you swipe a touch screen? And what does that cable sticking out of the TV actually do? The answers to all these questions are right here — just ask a member of the Computer Crew. These guys can put the world at your fingertips.

Microchip

⭐ Brain Box

THE BIG IDEA

A group of mini circuits (see page 28) inside a **device**. It tells the device what to do when it receives a command.

If you've ever used an electronic device, you should know that I'm the one doing most of the work. I'm Microchip, the brains inside a gadget. But what's inside me? A lot of circuits is the easy answer, and I use them to send signals around a device.

Small and flat, I'm made of silicon, a chemical element found in sand. I'm super tiny, too — just a fraction of an inch (a couple of millimeters) across — and some gizmos have several microchips inside them. I just need to be coded so that I can pass on my instructions to other Computer Crew members: Computer, Game Console, and Smartphone.

- ◉ Microchips can perform hundreds of billions of calculations a second

- ◉ Silicon is the second-most-common element in Earth's crust, after oxygen

- ◉ In 2013, scientists made a computer smaller than a grain of sand!

SAY WHAT?

Device: A piece of mechanical or electronic equipment used for a particular task, such as a cell phone or calculator.

TECH LEGEND

American computer scientist Grace Hopper is often called the "mother of computing." In the 1950s, she developed one of the first modern programming languages that allowed us to talk to computers in code.

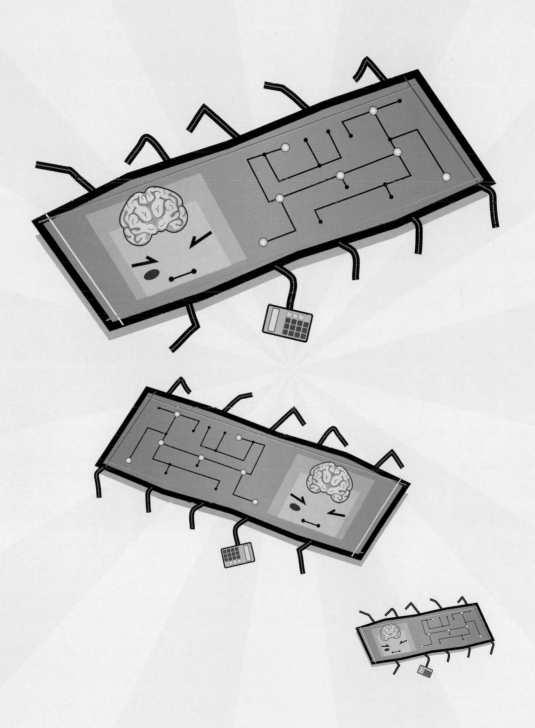

Circuit

⭐ Power Pusher

THE BIG IDEA

A web of tiny wires used to channel electricity to the different parts of a device.

If Microchip is the brains inside a device, then I'm its beating heart: Circuit. I allow electricity to travel nonstop around Computer, Game Console, and Smartphone. I give these machines (and others) the power they need to operate.

I use a system of wires along which tiny particles called **electrons** flow as electric current. Different parts of a machine switch on or off depending on when my current reaches them. Sure, Battery and Generator provide the power, but I deliver it where it's needed.

- Electrons create a flow of charge, which we call electricity

- Electrons always flow from negative to positive in a circuit

- Electricity travels at about 90% of the speed of light

SAY WHAT?

Electron: A tiny particle (see page 8) with a negative electric charge. Electrons are used to transfer power in a circuit.

APPLYING SCIENCE

A circuit uses one of two types of current: alternating current (AC) or direct current (DC). AC allows you to change power levels and is good for supplying electricity to the home. DC provides a constant current and is used in things like batteries.

Cable

⭐ Mega Connector

THE BIG IDEA

A collection of wires bundled together inside a flexible tube. It is used to transfer power or information between two things.

So you have a gadget — say, a lamp — and you have a plug, but how useful are they without me, Cable? I may just be a bunch of wires wrapped in rubber, but you need me to get electric current to flow from your plug to your light. Otherwise you'll have to stay in the dark.

You'll see me everywhere at home, but I'm used elsewhere, too. I bring electricity from the power plant to your house, for starters. And I don't just carry power — oh no. I can also transfer **data**. For example, it's me that transfers video games from Game Console to Television!

- A basic form of power cable was made by Thomas Edison in 1882

- One of the world's longest power cables is underwater and is 360 miles (580 km) long; it carries electrical power between Norway and the Netherlands

APPLYING SCIENCE

While regular cables use wires, fiber-optic cables use light to transfer data in larger amounts. We use these cables for high-speed Internet.

Computer
⭐ Master of All

THE BIG IDEA

A device for working with information (numbers, words, pictures, or sounds). Computer information is called data.

Wow! I'm Computer. You're going to think I'm complicated, but you know a good deal about me already. First, I'm rammed with fellow crew members Microchip and Circuit. They help me operate. Second, I have a screen that is just like TV's. It uses pixels to display things that you want to see.

What you might not know is that I store data on my **hard drive**. You give me an instruction using my keyboard or trackpad, and I'll access my data to perform the task. Just like you, I store my information as memory. When I use it, my activity is called processing. Go on, ask me to do something! Anything!

◉ The world's most powerful computer is a supercomputer called Summit

◉ More than two billion personal computers are currently in use around the world

SAY WHAT?

Hard drive: Equipment that stores data as memory. It can be in the form of a spinning disk or a group of circuits.

TECH LEGEND

The world's first modern computer was conceived by British mathematician Charles Babbage in the 1800s. His design measured more than 9.5 ft. x 6.5 ft. (3 m x 2 m) and did not use electricity, but it was never finished.

Game Console

⭐ Player One

THE BIG IDEA

A computer system that connects to a television and is used for playing video games.

Remember Television, the "great entertainer"? Don't make me laugh! Sure, its screen comes in handy, but I bring the real action to the party. With me, Game Console, you can have superpowers or travel to faraway lands. And you don't even have to leave your couch.

Like Computer, I'm all chips and circuits on the inside. Graphic chips help create a world for you to explore. Input chips let you control a character while you're there. Just use Cable to connect me to Television, work your way through my simple **interface**, and off you go! Happy travels!

- ◉ More than two billion people in the world play video games

- ◉ The global gaming industry is worth about $135 billion

- ◉ The top-selling games of all time include *Tetris* and *Minecraft*

SAY WHAT?

Interface: A system of menus that allows you to use a computer or game console. You make selections using a controller.

TECH LEGEND

American Ralph Baer released the first game console in 1972. It was called the Magnavox Odyssey. The games were simple and mostly involved moving squares of light on the screen. Games included tennis and football.

Touch Screen

★ Display Changer

THE BIG IDEA

A screen that you interact with by using your fingers instead of a mouse or a keyboard.

Yeah, yeah, I've heard enough from Microchip and Circuit. Let's talk about me, Touch Screen, the smooth face of Smartphone. Give me the slightest tap, swipe, or scroll, and I'll zap info right at you.

How do I do it? Well, I use sneaky science, that's how. In most cases, my changing display relies on something called "**capacitive** touch." That's a fancy way of saying I use the electricity in your body to know when you're touching me. Yes, you're electric! Don't believe me? Just try getting me to work for you when you're wearing gloves.

- ◉ The world's first touch screen was invented in 1965

- ◉ Some screens can use cameras to read your movements

- ◉ The record speed for waterskiing while texting is 16 mph (25 kmh)!

SAY WHAT?

Capacitance: The word for how circuits and other things store electricity as electric charge. In touch screens, the thing storing the charge is you!

SCIENCE NOW

Some touch screens use "haptic" technology. This involves tiny mechanisms behind a screen that react to your touch! They can give you the sensation that you're touching a different surface, such as sand or water.

Smartphone
★ Pocket Pal

THE BIG IDEA

A handheld device that uses a small computer and an Internet connection to perform a range of tasks.

Smart by name and smart by nature, I'm Smartphone, a pocket-size computer with a huge range of functions. You can use me to call or text your friends, and to interact with them using social media via Internet. I'll also let you store and play music, take selfies, play video games — oh, and so much more.

My pal Touch Screen will help you do things using my operating system. And, of course, I rely on Microchip and Circuit to carry those things out. Most of the time my energy comes from Battery, and I use Cable to charge it up when running low. Super smart, no?

- ◉ More than three billion people in the world use a smartphone

- ◉ The most popular **operating system** is Google's Android

- ◉ A tablet is like a big smartphone without the phone element

SAY WHAT?

Operating system: A program inside a computer that controls all its basic functions.

TECH LEGEND

American businesswoman Donna Dubinsky developed an early smartphone in 1995. It was called a "personal digital assistant" (PDA). Although it was bulkier than our phones today, it made modern smartphone technology possible.

Internet

⭐ World Wide Wizard

THE BIG IDEA

The worldwide system of interconnected computer **networks**, all sharing information on a global scale.

Simply awesome, I'm Internet, the incredible system that links billions of computers, smartphones, tablets, and an ever-increasing number of other devices around the world.

Together, they share data with each other so that you have practically all the information you could ever possibly need at your fingertips. Say you want to know how to bake chocolate muffins, or to find out the time in Tokyo, or to watch the latest SpaceX launch. Yep, just ask a search engine, and I'll come up with the goods in no time.

⊙ The world's first website was created in 1990

⊙ China has the most Internet users of any country

⊙ The first video on YouTube was uploaded in 2005

SAY WHAT?

Network: In computing, a system that connects any number of devices to each other so they can communicate with each other.

APPLYING SCIENCE

Computers all play by the same rules, which we call the Internet Protocol (IP). To make things easy to see, we use the World Wide Web (WWW). This is the language our computers use to talk to each other.

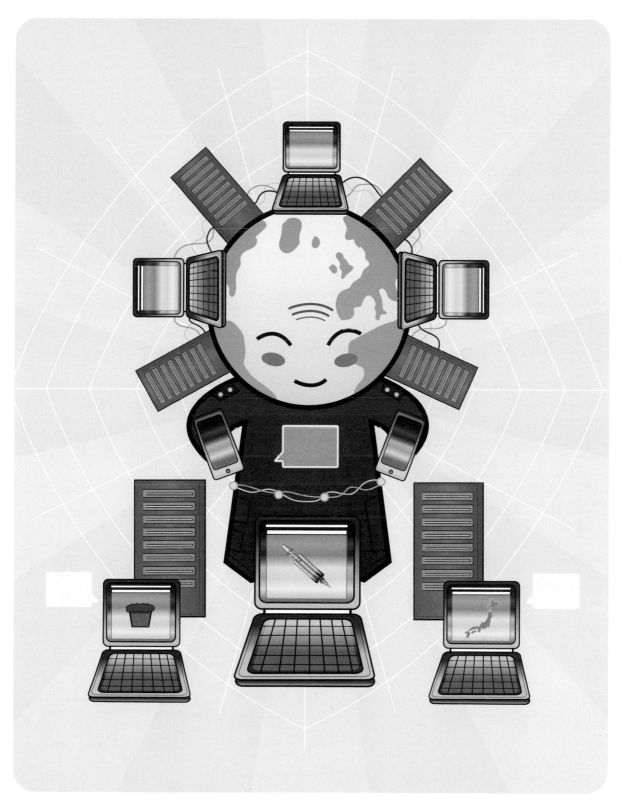

Wi-Fi

★ Wireless Wonder

THE BIG IDEA

A method that connects two or more devices to each other and/or the Internet without using wires.

Ha! I'm Wi-Fi, the last word in connectivity: no tangles, no trips, and freedom to roam. My pal Cable is *sooo* last century!

So I'm "wireless." I'm a whiz at getting you onto the Internet no matter where you happen to be. I don't need Cable to transfer information from one device to another. Instead, I turn data into a **signal** and use clever Radio's waves to send it through thin air. All Computer needs to do is collect my waves and change them back into useful information.

SAY WHAT?

Signal: This is a radio wave that is sent or received between two devices, such as the signals your TV receives to play shows.

- The world-record Wi-Fi distance for sending data is 436 miles (702 km)

- Some companies are trying to beam Internet to Earth from space

- "Wi-Fi" doesn't mean anything. People used it because it sounds cool!

TECH LEGEND

Wi-Fi was invented by Australian astronomer John O'Sullivan in the 1990s. He was actually looking for mini black holes. He accidentally discovered a way to send radio waves instead, and this led to the happy creation of Wi-Fi.

Bar Code

Radar

Laser

Satellite

Virtual Reality

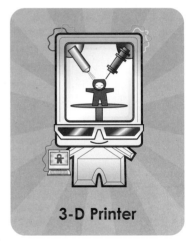

3-D Printer

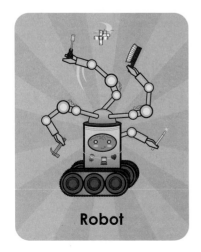

Robot

Artificial Intelligence

Super High-Tech Crew

Think of the coolest technology in the world,
and it probably belongs to the Super High-Tech Crew.
This is where Robot and Artifical Intelligence hang
out, taking on tasks that humans might do. Also going
the distance are Laser, Radar, and Satellite. If you
think Satellite is out of this world, wait until you meet
Virtual Reality. That's a different world altogether!

Bar Code
★ Super Scanner

THE BIG IDEA

A pattern of black-and-white lines that gives an item a unique number that a machine can read.

You're buying some new shoes and they're in a box. The cashier waves the box in front of a scanner at the register, and the machine knows what's in the box. How come? That's because what the cashier actually **scanned** was me: Bar Code!

I'm a series of black-and-white "bars" that represent numbers. Each number from 0 to 9 has a certain pattern of bars. The numbers themselves stand for information. The scanner scans my bars and changes them into numbers so Computer knows exactly what it's dealing with.

- ◉ The bar code was invented by two Americans in 1951

- ◉ Bar codes were used for freight trains before they were used in stores; railroad cars were scanned arriving at and leaving freight yards

SAY WHAT?

Scanning: Using a laser beam to read a bar code so that information can be processed by a computer.

SCIENCE NOW

A Quick Response (QR) code is a more modern type of bar code. A small square with black-and-white dots, it contains more information and can be scanned by a smartphone camera. QR codes can be used to provide information on museum tours and in other places of interest.

Radar

★ Pinpoint Locator

THE BIG IDEA

A way of tracking the location and speed of an airplane or car by bouncing radio waves off it.

When a plane travels through the air, how do you know where it is? Ask me, Radar. I can show you. Remember Radio on page 18? I use Radio's waves to locate things such as aircraft in the sky.

Usually a big dish on the ground, I fire my waves into the air. They travel at the speed of light, which is about 190,000 miles (300,000 km) per second! When they hit something, they just bounce back. By measuring the time it takes for the waves to return, operators can figure out exactly where the plane is and the speed at which it is traveling.

⊙ An early form of **radar** was called the Telemobiloscope (1904)

⊙ Modern radar helped spot enemy planes during World War II

⊙ Radar is used in space exploration to study other worlds

SAY WHAT?

Radar: The word radar is made up from the first letters of the words **ra**dio **d**etection **a**nd **r**anging.

REAL-WORLD VIEW

Sometimes police officers use a radar gun to see if a car is speeding. The faster a car travels, the more it makes the radio waves stretch out when they bounce back. This is called the Doppler effect.

Laser
★ Beam Buddy

THE BIG IDEA

A concentrated ray of light that's often fired down and out of a narrow tube. The beam can be one of many different colors.

You may know me from the movies, but I'm a science legend, too! I'm Laser, and I like to reveal myself as a mega-powerful beam of light.

I'm made up of light that's squashed really tightly together in some sort of tube, like a laser pen. This makes my atoms get excited, and they release even more particles of light. Firing my light out of a narrow opening keeps it focused in a completely straight beam that can travel over large distances. Best of all, I come in a range of fab colors, depending on the atoms used to make me.

- The first laser was made in 1960 using a ruby

- Lasers are used for reading DVDs

- Scientists use lasers to measure distances in space

SAY WHAT?

Laser: The word laser is made up of the first letters of the words **l**ight **a**mplification by **s**timulated **e**mission of **r**adiation.

＊ REAL-WORLD VIEW ＊

Lasers are used all the time, but you might not know it. They carry TV and Internet signals, for example, because they can travel great distances. They are also used for the precision cutting of metal and even your clothes!

Satellite
★ Awesome Orbiter

THE BIG IDEA

A space-based machine that travels around Earth, gathering information and aiding communication.

Hi, I'm Satellite, and I'm outta this world. No, really! I'm one of those funky machines located way above your head. Out in space, I **orbit** Earth at mega-high speeds. Earth's **gravity** tries to draw me in, but I move so fast that I always stay on my path.

I come in many shapes and sizes. Some are as small as a toaster, while others are bigger than a car! I send signals all over the planet, such as TV shows. I can also take pictures of Earth and even watch the planet's weather. I'm a multitalented type, that's for sure!

- There are about 5,000 satellites orbiting Earth today, although some don't work anymore

- Most satellites use solar panels to power themselves

SAY WHAT?

Orbit: The path a satellite takes around a planet.

Gravity: A force that attracts objects toward each other.

* APPLYING SCIENCE *

The first satellite was Sputnik 1, launched by the Soviet Union (now Russia) in 1957. It sparked a space race between the Soviet Union and the United States. The U.S. won when it landed men on the Moon in 1969!

Virtual Reality

★ World Builder

THE BIG IDEA

Using a screen as part of a **headset**, this technology can transport you to another location.

I take entertainment to the next level, helping you escape the comfort of your own home and travel my magical world of adventure! I'm Virtual Reality. Want to borrow my headset? Sure, try it on for size.

That screen in front of your eyes can send you to far-flung and extraordinary places, from the depths of an ocean to the surface of an alien planet. Move your head and you'll see that the headset tracks your motion. Now you're ready to explore the world you are in, playing games, rising to challenges, and learning new skills.

- ◉ NASA uses virtual reality to train its astronauts to space walk

- ◉ As many as four million virtual reality headsets were sold in 2018

SAY WHAT?

Headset: In virtual reality, a device worn over the face. It places a screen in front of the eyes that makes the wearer feel as if they have stepped into a new world.

SCIENCE NOW

"Augmented reality" uses a device to make virtual things appear in the real world. You might have used this on a smartphone, selecting filters to add funny hats and glasses to your face when taking selfies.

3-D Printer

★ Shape Maker

You will have seen a regular printer in action — the kind that uses ink to make words and pictures appear on a page. Now imagine something similar happening, but building layer upon layer, in a stack. Can such a thing be possible? Yes, because that is exactly what I do: I'm 3-D Printer.

Taking instructions from Computer, I print in layers to make a solid, **3-D** shape. I use plastic, not ink, to work my magic. These days I am mostly used for printing models for designers, but soon I could be printing objects for you in your home!

- ◉ The first modern 3-D printer was invented in 1988

- ◉ Some machines use 3-D printing to build entire houses

- ◉ In the future we might all have a 3-D printer at home

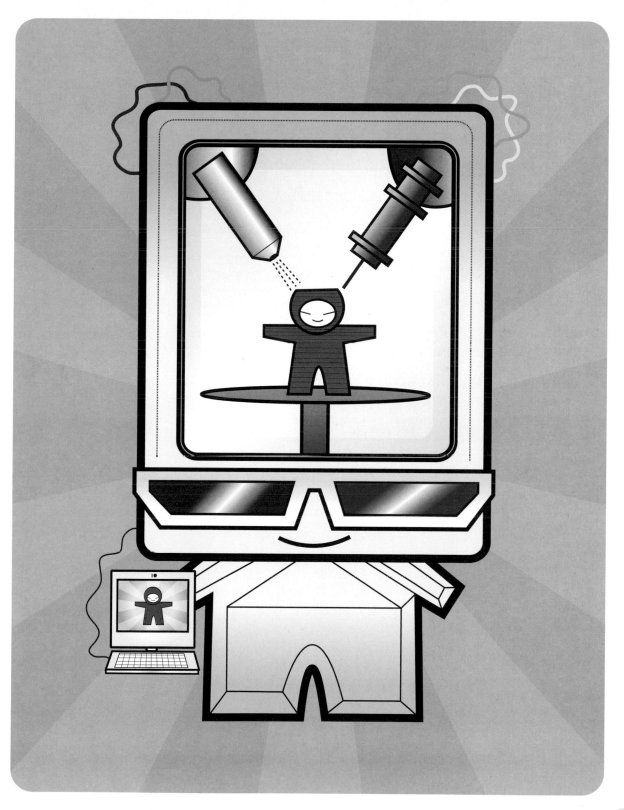

Robot

★ Mechanical Human

THE BIG IDEA

A machine that can perform tasks a human might do, such as making things or walking around.

Hello, I'm Robot, and I am any machine that has been designed to perform a task a human can do. Sometimes I even look almost human, in which case I am also known as an **android**.

Computer acts as my brain, and I take my energy from Battery, or another electricity source, so I never get tired. That makes me popular in factories: I'm happy to work around the clock. I often have movable parts — mechanical arms or legs, for example — and am used for all sorts of things, from building cars to harvesting crops to vacuuming rooms.

● A robot was sent to the International Space Station in 2011 to see how well robots can work in space

● Doctors sometimes use robots to help them perform surgery

SAY WHAT?

Android: A robot that is in the shape of a human. It has legs and arms that can move, just like your own limbs.

TECH LEGEND

ASIMO, created by Japanese manufacturer Honda in 2000, was one of the world's first androids. It could walk on two legs and even talk! Today ASIMO is in a museum, but it used to tour the world!

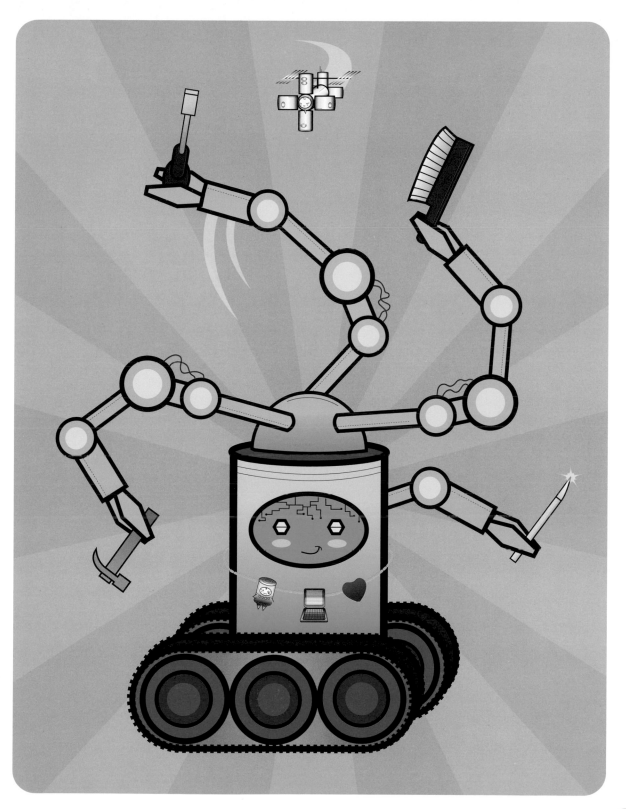

Artificial Intelligence

★ Electric Brain

THE BIG IDEA

A machine or computer program that can solve things by itself. It is more commonly known as AI.

Watch out, I'm Artificial Intelligence! Some people find me a little spooky, because I'm not that different from the brain inside your head. You can call me AI!

Like Computer, I rely on Microchip and Circuit to help me function. But Computer needs to be programmed, while I can work things out for myself. Start me off with a little basic knowledge and I'll build on it over time, just like you do at school. You might have an AI **smart device** or two at home. Ask the device a question and the AI will try to figure out the answer. Smart thinking, no?

⚡ **SAY WHAT?** ⚡

Smart device: A small machine with AI. The AI can perform basic tasks, such as checking the weather or doing some shopping.

＊ **FAST-FORWARD** ＊

Some people think AI will rival the human brain in the future. Others are looking at ways of combining humans and AI, to make humans that are even smarter!

◉ In 1997, AI computer Deep Blue beat the world's best chess player

◉ AI is used in many ways, from smart speakers to self-driving cars to making reservations in restaurants

Generator

Fuel Cell

Transmission Tower

Solar Power

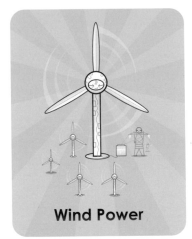

Wind Power

Geothermal Power

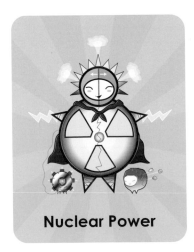

Nuclear Power

Fusion Power

Power Pals

Thinking of flicking a switch in your house? You'll probably need help from one of us — your Power Pals! We let you turn on your lights or watch TV! There is no end to our wizardry. While some of us have been around for centuries, others, such as Fusion Power, are still very young. It's time to learn more about power from the past, present . . . and future.

Generator

★ Super Spinner

THE BIG IDEA

A machine that can be used to produce electricity by spinning a wire between two magnets.

See my name, Generator? I *generate* electricity. At my heart are two magnets and, between them, a metal wire. The magnets face each other north pole to south pole (opposites attract, you know). The magnets pull on each other, creating a magnetic field.

All I need now is to get my wire spinning. When that happens inside a magnetic field, it creates electricity. Power plants heat water to produce steam, which spins the wire using a **turbine**. Another kind of turbine uses my pal Wind Power to spin my wire. Feeling dizzy?

- ◉ The first generators for producing a steady electric current were invented in the 1830s.

- ◉ The world's biggest generator is the Three Gorges Dam in China

SAY WHAT?

Magnetic field: The area near a magnet within which the force of the magnet can be felt either pulling or pushing.
Turbine: A machine in which a rotor revolves to produce power.

✳ APPLYING SCIENCE ✳

Scientists look for sources of energy that don't harm the environment. When oil burns, it produces polluting carbon dioxide. It is much better to use cleaner, "greener" energy sources such as wind and the Sun.

Fuel Cell

★ Hydrogen Charger

THE BIG IDEA

A type of battery that uses **hydrogen** to produce electricity. It strips hydrogen atoms of their electrons to make a charge.

Remember Battery? Well, what if there was a greener, cleaner, more energy-giving alternative? You guessed it, there is — me! I'm Fuel Cell. I'm a little like Battery, but I have hydrogen atoms inside me instead of a chemical. I'm green because I generate energy rather than just storing it!

Hydrogen atoms lose their electrons when they're inside me. Electrons are particles that orbit the center of an atom. They can be used to produce electricity because they have a negative charge. All *power* to me! Adding oxygen to the mix turns the leftover hydrogen into water. That makes me clean!

- ◉ Hydrogen fuel cells are used in cars and even spacecraft

- ◉ Hydrogen can be made by splitting water into hydrogen and oxygen

SAY WHAT?

Hydrogen: The most common element in the universe. It is also the element with the fewest particles.

TECH LEGEND

Welsh physicist William Grove first came up with the idea for fuel cells in 1838. His idea wasn't refined until the 20th century, when scientists realized how useful it could be.

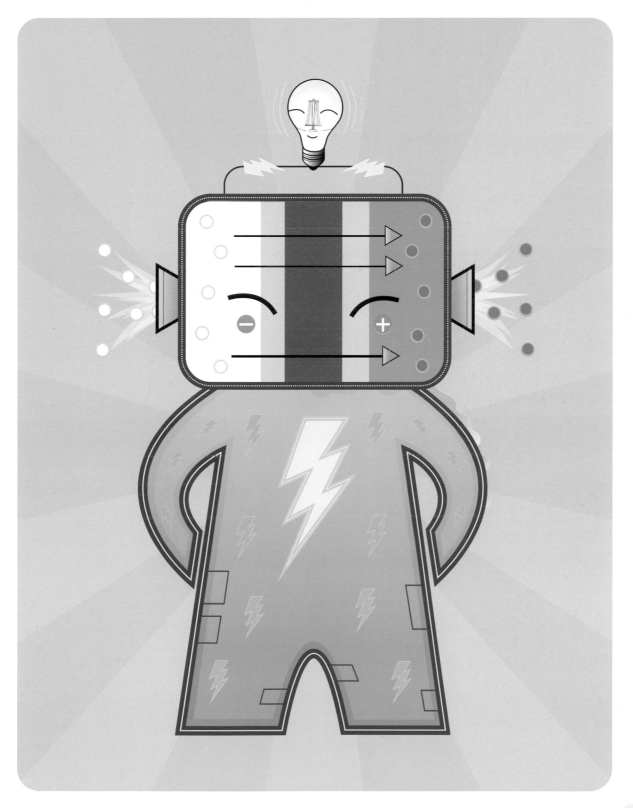

Transmission Tower

★ Electric Transporter

THE BIG IDEA

A large metal structure for suspending cables that are used for transporting electricity.

Got some electricity you want to move? Let me bring it from the power plant to your home. I'm Transmission Tower, a big metal structure with Cable running over me. You'll see hundreds of my type stretching across the landscape. Passing Cable from one of us to the next, we cover great distances.

Of course, Cable is tough enough to carry the high-**voltage** electricity that leaves the power plant. But that electricity is powerful stuff, so I use something called a transformer to lower the voltage before sending it into your home.

⊙ The world's two tallest transmission towers are at Ningbo-Zhoushan Port, east China; they measure 1,245 ft. (380 m) tall.

⊙ In some countries transmission towers are called "pylons"

SAY WHAT?

Voltage: Almost like pressure, this is a measure of the difference in electric potential between two points. The higher the voltage, the more electricity is available.

FAST-FORWARD

There are ideas for making transmission towers better looking! These include one design that resembles a giant sail and another that is T-shaped with two ends for holding cables — like hanging baskets.

Solar Power

★ Sun Collector

THE BIG IDEA

Harnessing energy from the Sun to generate electricity.

Sunlight is made of tiny particles called **photons**, which rain down on Earth all the time. I'm Solar Power, and my trick is to turn that sunlight into electricity. Well, it's there for the taking, isn't it?

All I need to do is catch the photons. That's where an electrical device called a solar cell comes in handy. When photons hit my solar cell, they cause an electric current to run through it. Sure, it's a small amount of electricity, but it increases quickly if I use a good number of solar cells alongside each other in solar panels. Not only that, but it's really clean. Win-win!

◉ Solar cells are normally made from silicon, found in sand

◉ The Tengger Desert Solar Park in China is the world's largest solar farm. Covering 16.6 m² (43 km²), it has the same area as almost 165,000 tennis courts

SAY WHAT?

Photon: A tiny particle of energy that makes up all light. Photons travel at a top speed of more than 671 million mph (1 billion kmh), the speed of light.

✳ APPLYING SCIENCE ✳

In just one hour, enough sunlight hits Earth to power the entire planet for a year! Thanks to solar panels, we can use sunlight to power people's houses — and to power satellites orbiting Earth, too.

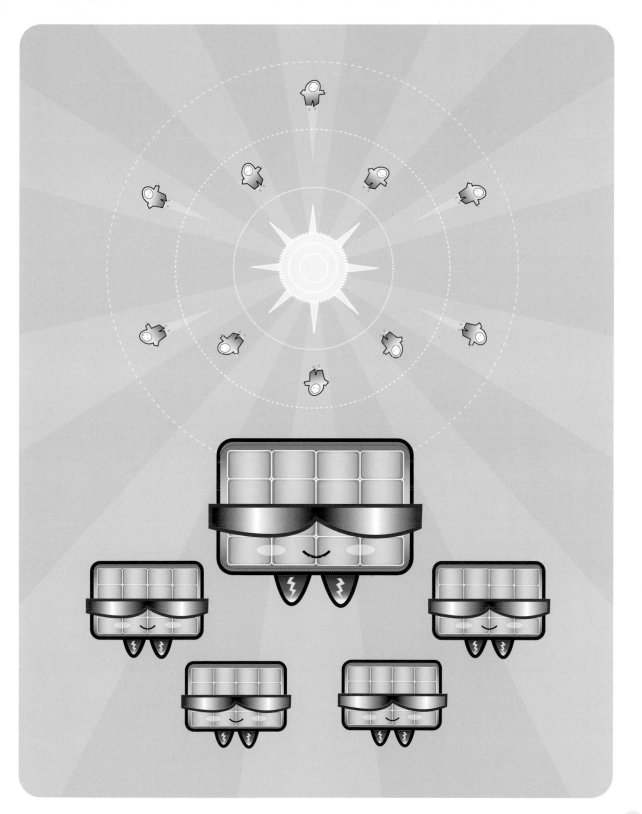

Wind Power

★ Rad Rotator

THE BIG IDEA
Harnessing energy from the wind to generate electricity.

Hi, I'm Wind Power. If you're out looking for Transmission Tower, you might spot my wind turbines — huge windmills with tall, strong poles topped with rotary blades. They dot the landscape and can sometimes be seen wading out at sea.

When wind **rotates** the blades, it also turns Generator inside the top of my pole. This produces electricity that can be used to power lots of things, including your house. The faster the wind blows, the faster the blades rotate and the more electricity is produced. But don't expect me to be busy on calm days. No, you'll need Battery for those!

- The largest wind turbines generate power for up to 3,000 homes each

- There are around 350,000 wind turbines on Earth

SAY WHAT?

Rotate: To travel in a circular motion around a central point.

SCIENCE NOW

The blades of a windmill operate in much the same way as an airplane's wings. When a plane moves forward, wind rushes under its wings and produces lift. When the wind blows windmill blades, they rotate around instead of going up!

Geothermal Power

★ Hot Stuff

THE BIG IDEA

Harnessing energy from underground hot water and steam to generate electricity.

You might not know this, but I am a totally natural source of power found right beneath your feet. Yes, I'm Geothermal Power, and I bring you hot water and steam from underground! Not impressed? Well, I can replace oil and gas when it comes to driving Generator's turbine, and that makes me an environmental hero.

My heat comes from inside Earth. You see, Earth is really, really hot at its core, or center — 11,230°F (6,000°C)! As the heat radiates out and up, it heats water below the surface, creating steam. Wow, it sure is toasty in here . . .

- ◉ "Geothermal" comes from the Greek *geo* (Earth) and *therme* (heat)

- ◉ The first geothermal power plant was built in Larderello, Italy, in 1904

- ◉ Geothermal power generates 25% of Iceland's electricity

⚡ SAY WHAT? ⚡

Celsius: A temperature scale, measured in degrees (°): 0°C is the freezing point of water; 100°C is water's boiling point.

✳ APPLYING SCIENCE ✳

Heat from Earth's core also powers volcanoes! The heat is so intense that it can melt rocks, turning them into a hot liquid called magma. When magma spews out of an erupting volcano, it is called lava.

Nuclear Power

★ Atom Smasher

THE BIG IDEA

Harnessing the energy from splitting, or breaking, atoms apart to generate power.

You already know that atoms make up the entire universe. And that atoms themselves are made up of even tinier particles — protons, electrons, and **neutrons**. Well, if you break an atom apart using a powerful machine, it can be used to produce me — Nuclear Power.

Nuclear power plants split atoms of an element called uranium. This produces heat, which is used to turn water into steam and . . . you know where I'm going with this? Yep! The steam powers a turbine to turn my friend Generator, and presto: electricity!

- There are around 450 nuclear power plants in the world

- Nuclear power plants produce about 11% of the world's electricity

SAY WHAT?

Neutron: Along with protons and electrons, neutrons are one of the three key particles found inside atoms.

SCIENCE NOW

Nuclear power produces a lot of high-energy waves or particles (radiation) that can move through things easily. Large amounts of radiation can be harmful to humans. Fortunately, nuclear power plants are very safe.

Fusion Power
★ Star Struck

THE BIG IDEA

Harnessing the energy from fusing, or joining, atoms together to generate power.

Don't confuse me with boring old Nuclear Power. That's called fission, but I'm Fusion Power, the energy-releasing activity at the center of **stars** such as the Sun. I involve the mega-hot process of fusing hydrogen atoms together to create HUGE amounts of energy. How else could the Sun be so bright?

The problem is that fusion is difficult to recreate, and scientists have not quite got the hang of it yet. So you could say I'm a potential energy source for the future: clean, energetic, and powerful.

- ◉ The first fusion power plant may get going in the 2030s
- ◉ Some people hope fusion will one day power the entire world

SAY WHAT?

Star: A giant ball of gas found in space. It's so big that it squashes atoms together inside, which makes it get very hot.

REAL-WORLD VIEW

A number of fusion power experiments are underway in China, Germany, South Korea, and elsewhere. They involve research where temperatures are as hot as the Sun.

Sail

Combustion Engine

Jet Engine

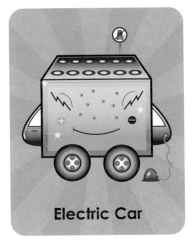

Electric Car

Maglev Train

Rocket

Turbo Transporters

These amazing vehicles allow you to travel the world —
and beyond! Have you ever wondered what powers a
car? Or how a sail helps a boat move? What keeps an
airplane in the sky? You'll find all the answers to these
questions on the following pages, but there's more!
If you dream of space travel, won't you need a rocket
to get there? Turn the page and let these fun
characters tell you how to get from A to B.

Sail

★ Wind Rider

THE BIG IDEA

This method of transportation uses a large sheet to capture the force of the **wind** and propel a boat forward through water.

So you want to travel across the ocean? Let me help you! I'm Sail, an ancient way of using the wind to move your boat forward through the water!

I attach to a boat's mast — a tall pole that stands upright in the middle of the deck. Along my bottom edge, I often attach to a boom, another pole that sticks out at a right angle and can be swung around to change my position. I catch the wind when it blows, filling out with its force. I hold fast, resisting the wind, and the force transfers to the boat, driving it across the water!

- The largest present-day sailing ship, the *Royal Clipper*, has 42 sails

- A boat's speed is measured in knots; 1 knot is 1.15 mph (1.85 kmh)

SAY WHAT?

Wind: Moving air that's caused by a change in pressure in Earth's atmosphere. The bigger the change, the faster the wind.

✳ ANCIENT SAILORS ✳

Sailing is one of the oldest types of human transportation. It is thought that the first people to use sails lived in what is now Kuwait 7,000 years ago. The ancient Egyptians were using sails more than 5,000 years ago.

Combustion Engine

⭐ Fuel Friend

THE BIG IDEA

An engine in which fuel is burned to force parts of a machine to move, which then turn the wheels of a vehicle, such as a car.

Vrroom vrrroom! If you've ever heard a car go, then you've been listening to me, Combustion Engine! "Combustion" is just a fancy way of saying that I burn stuff, usually **gasoline** in air.

I burn fuel to create gases at high pressure. These force rods called pistons to move up and down. The action makes a crankshaft (another rod) go around. And a car's wheels are attached to the crankshaft. Watch them spin! Pressing a car's gas pedal sends more air and fuel my way, so I release more energy and the wheels spin faster. Pedal to the metal!

⦿ The world's first car was invented in 1886

⦿ There are more than one billion cars in the world

⦿ The word "car" comes from the Latin *carrus* (wheeled vehicle)

SAY WHAT?

Gasoline: A type of fuel that is made from petroleum (or oil) pumped out of the ground.

✳ SCIENCE NOW ✳

Combustion engines produce carbon dioxide and other pollutants, which are bad for the atmosphere. These days, electric cars are becoming more popular. They run on electricity and are much cleaner.

Jet Engine

★ Thrust Titan

THE BIG IDEA

This powerful piece of machinery burns fuel and air together to produce a large force that can push an airplane through the air.

If you've ever been on a plane, you've seen me in action! I'm Jet Engine, and I operate a little like Combustion Engine to turn fuel into a really powerful **thrust**.

Put fuel inside me, and I'll burn it with air to produce energy. The air comes in through a big fan at my front end. Burning it with fuel creates a huge amount of gas, which then gets fired out of my rear end! It's this action that drives the plane forward. With me on board, a plane can travel at around 500 mph (800 kmh). Whoosh!

◉ Between 8,000 and 20,000 planes are in the air at any given moment

◉ Four billion passengers took to the skies in 2018

SAY WHAT?

Thrust: The force produced by a jet engine as it moves an airplane through the air.

TECH LEGEND

We know how a jet engine works thanks to 17th-century British physicist Isaac Newton. In his laws of motion, he says that every action has an equal and opposite reaction. So when a jet engine fires gas backward, it also pushes the plane forward!

Electric Car

★ Clean Driver

THE BIG IDEA

A vehicle that runs on electricity and doesn't give off any harmful gases. It has a battery inside that can be recharged.

Hi, I'm Electric Car, and I'm one clean machine! I drive the wheels of a vehicle using an electric motor instead of an engine. With me on the roads, you can say goodbye to dirty old gas-guzzling Combustion Engine and make **pollution** a thing of the past.

My motor is powered by clever Battery — just plug me in to charge it up. A control unit inside me helps regulate the amount of power sent to the wheels. This lets the driver speed up and slow down easily. Hey, let's roll!

⦿ The most popular brands of electric cars in the United States are built by Tesla

⦿ Another type of clean car uses a fuel cell to drive its motor

SAY WHAT?

Pollution: Substances that damage an environment. A gasoline car's exhaust contains many substances that pollute Earth's atmosphere.

✳ REAL-WORLD VIEW ✳

Electric cars have been around for decades, but it's only recently that scientists have found a way to store a lot of energy inside batteries. An electric car can travel 150 miles (240 km) on a single charge.

Maglev Train
★ Magnetic Speedster

THE BIG IDEA

A train that uses very powerful magnets to hover above a track. The magnets push the train forward and also slow it down.

Look at me — I'm flying! No, really! You've seen hundreds of trains with wheels that run on rails. But not me, Maglev Train. I use really powerful **electromagnets** to hover a few inches or so above my metal track.

My name is short for "magnetic levitation" (that's floating to you and me). The magnets don't just make me float — they push me forward, too! I don't even have an engine. Of course, Battery powers the magnets, but other than that I'm as free as the wind (only faster). In tests, I have reached speeds of 375 mph (600 kmh). Catch me if you can!

◉ The first high-speed maglev train for passengers started operating in China in 2002

◉ Passenger maglev trains travel at about 200 mph (320 kmh)

SAY WHAT?

Electromagnet: A magnet made by running electricity through a coiled wire. The more coils, the stronger the magnet.

TECH LEGEND

German engineer Alfred Zehden came up with the idea of magnetic levitation in 1902, but it wasn't until 1979 that the first maglev train was built, in Hamburg, Germany.

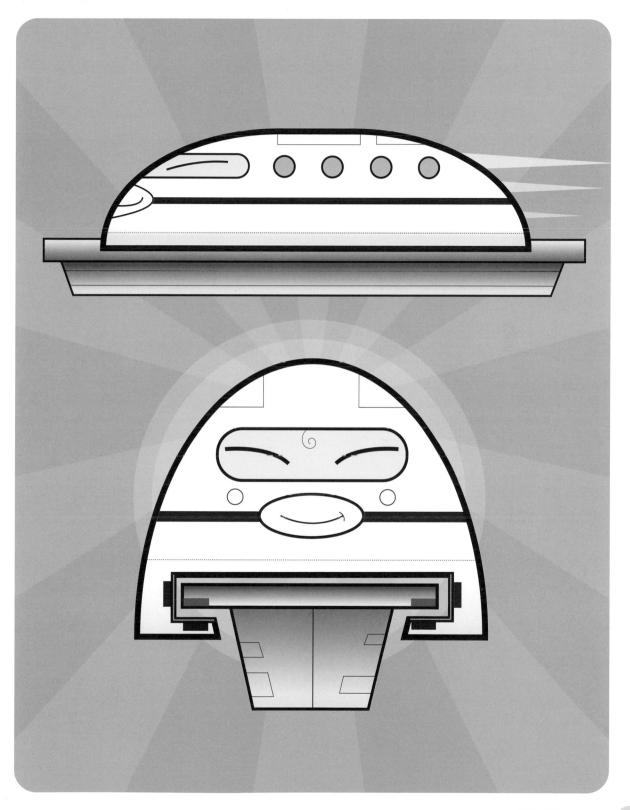

Rocket

★ Mega Launcher

THE BIG IDEA

A large vehicle that uses powerful engines to blast itself upward and into **space** above Earth.

I'm Rocket. Like Jet Engine, I have mega-powerful engines and burn fuel to generate thrust. But unlike Jet Engine, I carry everything I need for burning my fuel with me, so I don't need oxygen from the air. That means I can work in empty space!

Up, up, and up I go, way past any jet engines, and getting faster all the time. Once my fuel is spent, I ditch parts I no longer need, to make me lighter. Then, upon reaching space, I throw my cargo ahead of me so it can go and explore! This could be Satellite — or even a spacecraft with you inside it. Come fly with me!

- ◉ The boundary of space begins 62 miles (100 km) above Earth

- ◉ It can take just eight minutes for a spacecraft to reach space from Earth

- ◉ In February 2018, SpaceX launched a car into space!

TECH LEGEND

Katherine Johnson was a mathematician at NASA who figured out the best route to fly humans to the Moon in 1969. Her calculations were so good that she was asked to check the computer's calculations on other spaceflights.

Glossary

Android: A robot that is in the shape of a human. It has legs and arms that can move, just like your own limbs.

Antenna: A metal rod, wire, or dish that is used to send and receive radio waves. It turns signals into radio waves and back again.

Atom: A tiny piece of matter, made of even tinier particles called protons, neutrons, and electrons. Everything you see around you is made up of atoms.

Bacteria: Super-tiny living things that can be found everywhere. Some help you digest your food, some cause diseases, and others can make food go bad.

Capacitance: The word for how circuits and other things store electricity as electric charge. In touch screens, the thing storing the charge is you!

Celsius: A temperature scale, measured in degrees (°): 0°C is the freezing point of water; 100°C is water's boiling point.

Chemical: A substance that is made of matter, the stuff you see all around you in the universe. It can be a single element, such as oxygen, or two or more elements connected together.

Coolant: A liquid or gas that is used to remove heat from something. It can sometimes change between a liquid and gas by changing its pressure.

Data: In a computer, this is information stored as numbers called bytes. The computer uses data to work things out.

Device: A piece of mechanical or electronic equipment used for a particular task, such as a cell phone or calculator.

Electricity: A flow of charged particles that takes the form of a current in a circuit.

Electromagnet: A magnet made by running electricity through a coiled wire. The more coils, the stronger the magnet.

Electron: A tiny particle with a negative electrical charge. Electrons are used to transfer power or energy in a circuit.

Element: A substance made of just one kind of atom, such as iron, oxygen, or carbon.

Energy: This is the ability of something to do some work, such as move in a certain direction. Energy can be stored, or it can be put into action by something.

Fuel: A substance that can supply energy when it is burned.

Gasoline: A type of fuel that is made from petroleum (or oil) pumped out of the ground.

Gravity: A force that attracts objects toward each other.

Green energy: A source of energy that doesn't produce waste products, such as sunlight or wind.

Hard drive: Equipment that stores data as memory. It can be in the form of a spinning disk or a group of circuits.

Headset: In virtual reality, a device worn over the face. It places a screen in front of the eyes that makes the wearer feel as if they have stepped into a new world.

Hydrogen: The most common element in the universe. It is also the element with the fewest particles.

Interface: A system of menus that allows you to use a computer or game console. You make selections using a controller.

Internet: The global network of computers that allows us to communicate with each other and share information "online."

Laser: A narrow, concentrated beam of light that can measure distances and even cut metal.

Magnet: A material, usually a metal, that has its atoms ordered in a particular way to produce a magnetic field, which can then attract or repel other magnetic objects.

Magnetic field: The area near a magnet within which the force of the magnet can be felt either pulling or pushing.

Magnetron: A device that produces microwaves by making electrons interact with a wire.

Memory (computer): A physical way for computers to store data, often on a device such as a hard drive.

Network: In computing, a system that connects any number of devices to each other so they can communicate with each other.

Neutron: Along with protons and electrons, neutrons are one of the three key particles found inside atoms. They have no electrical charge.

Operating system: A program inside a computer that controls all its basic functions.

Orbit: The path a satellite takes around a planet.

Particle: All things are made up of tiny atoms. Inside each atom are even smaller particles called protons, neutrons, and electrons.

Photon: A tiny particle of energy that makes up all light. Photons travel at a top speed of more than 671 million mph (1 billion kph), the speed of light.

Pixel: A tiny part of a display that can change color. Many pixels combine to make a larger picture.

Pollution: Substances that damage an environment. A gasoline car's exhaust contains many substances that pollute Earth's atmosphere.

Processing (computer): How a computer does things by executing commands, often inputted by a user.

Proton: A tiny particle found inside an atom. It has a positive electrical charge.

Radar: A way of tracking the speed and location of an object by bouncing radio waves off it.

Radiation: Energy that moves from one place to another. It is described as traveling in "waves."

Radio waves: A type of radiation that has a long distance between its waves, good for traveling over vast distances.

Rotate: To travel in a circular motion around a central point.

Scanning: Using a laser beam to read a bar code so that information can be processed by a computer.

Sewer: A network of large pipes that carries household waste to a place where it can be safely gotten rid of.

Signal: This is a radio wave that is sent or received between two devices, such as the signals your TV receives to play shows.

Smart device: A small machine with AI. The AI can perform basic tasks, such as checking the weather or doing some shopping.

Space: The mostly empty region between all planets and stars. It has no air, but many things can travel through it.

Star: A giant ball of gas found in space. It's so big that it squashes atoms together inside, which makes it get very hot.

3-D: The "three dimensions" that make up the world around us: length (or width), height, and depth.

Thrust: The force produced by a jet engine as it moves an airplane through the air.

Transformer: Something that can increase or reduce voltage between circuits. It can be used to send electrical power to your house in a safer form.

Transmitter: A device that uses a metal rod or wire called an antenna to send out radio waves. A radio set uses another antenna to receive the signals.

Turbine: A machine in which a rotor revolves to produce power.

Voltage: A measure of the difference in electric potential between two points. The higher the voltage, the more electricity is available.

Index

A
airplane 48, 86
alternating current (AC) 28
android 58, 94
antenna 18, 94
Artificial Intelligence (AI) **60–61**
ASIMO 58
atom 8, 12, 16, 50, 66, 76, 78, 94
augmented reality 54

B
bacteria 14, 94
Bar Code **46–47**
Battery **12–13**, 28, 38, 58, 66, 72, 88, 90
boat 82
byte 30

C
Cable **30–31**, 34, 38, 42, 68
capacitance 36, 94
car 12, 60, 66, 84, 88, 92
carbon dioxide 84
cell phone 16, 26
  see also Smartphone
Celsius scale 74, 94
Circuit 12, 20, 26, **28–29**, 32, 34, 36, 38, 60, 68
Combustion Engine **84–85**, 88
Computer 26, 28, **32–33**, 34, 38, 40, 42, 46, 56, 58, 60

D
data 30, 32, 40, 42, 94
Deep Blue 60
direct current (DC) 28
Doppler effect 48
DVD 50

E
Electric Car 84, **88–89**
electricity 8, 12, 16, 28, 30, 36, 64, 66, 68, 70, 72, 74, 76, 88, 90, 94
electromagnet 90
electron 8, 28, 66, 76, 94

F
fiber-optic cable 30
filament 8
fission 78
Fuel Cell **66–67**, 88
Fusion Power **78–79**

G
Game Console 26, 28, 30, **34–35**
gasoline 84, 95
Generator 28, **64–65**, 76

Geothermal Power **74–75**
gravity 52, 94
green energy 64, 66, 94

H
haptic technology 36
hard drive 32, 94
headset 54, 94
hydrogen 66, 78, 94

I
interface 34, 94
International Space Station 56, 58
Internet 22, 30, 38, **40–41**, 42, 50, 94
Internet of Things **22–23**
Internet Protocol (IP) 40

J
Jet Engine **86–87**

K
knot (speed) 82

L
Laser 46, **50–51**, 94
laws of motion 86
LCD (liquid crystal display) 20
LED (light-emitting diode) 8
Light Bulb **8–9**

M
Maglev Train **90–91**
magnet 64, 90, 95
magnetic field 64, 95
magnetron 16, 95
Microchip **26–27**, 32, 34, 38, 60
Microwave Oven **16–17**

N
network 40, 95
neutron 76, 95
Nuclear Power **76–77**

O
operating system 38, 95
orbit 52, 95
oxygen 26, 66

P
personal digital assistant (PDA) 38
photon 8, 70, 76, 95
pixel 20, 32, 95
pollution 88, 95
processing 32, 95

Q
Quick Response (QR) code 46

R
Radar 16, **48–49**, 95
radiation 16, 18, 50, 76, 95
Radio 16, **18–19**, 42, 48

Refrigerator **14–15**
Robot **58–59**
Rocket **92–93**

S
Sail **82–83**
Satellite 18, **52–53**, 70, 92
scanning 46, 95
search engine 40
sewer 10, 95
signal 42, 50, 52, 95
silicon 26, 70
smart device 60, 95
Smartphone 26, 28, 36, **38–39**, 40, 46, 54
solar cell 70
Solar Power 52, **70–71**
space 48, 50, 52, 54, 56, 58, 92, 95
speed camera 16
star 78, 95
supercomputer 32
surgery 58

T
tablet 38, 40
Television **20–21**, 30, 34, 42, 50, 52
3-D Printer **56–57**
thrust 86, 95
Toilet **10–11**
Touch Screen **36–37**, 38
train 90
transformer 68, 95
Transmission Tower **68–69**
transmitter 18, 95
turbine 64, 72, 74, 76, 95

U
uranium 76

V
Virtual Reality **54–55**
volcano 74
voltage 68, 95

W
Wi-Fi **42–43**
Wind Power 64, **72–73**, 82
windmill 72
World Wide Web 22

X
X-ray 16

Y
YouTube 40